The Complete Junior Guitarist

by Joe Bennett

Amsco Publications
part of The Music Sales Group
London/New York/Paris/Sydney/Copenhagen/Berlin/Madrid/Tokyo

Published by

Amsco Publications
257 Park Avenue South, New York, NY 10010, USA.

Exclusive Distributors in the USA, Canada, Mexico, and U.S. possessions:

Hal Leonard Corporation
7777 West Bluemound Road, Milwaukee, WI 53213, USA.

Exclusive Distributors for the rest of the World:

Music Sales Limited
Distribution Centre, Newmarket Road, Bury St Edmunds, Suffolk IP33 3YB, UK.

Music Sales Pty Limited
20 Resolution Drive, Caringbah, NSW 2229, Australia.

Order No: AM999581
ISBN: 978-0-8256-3738-4
HL Item Number: 14037550

Musical examples composed by Joe Bennett
Edited by Ann Barkway

Music processed by Paul Ewers Music Design
Photography: Matthew Ward and Simon Troup
Models: Mario Marin-borquez, Molly Lee, Poppy Troup, Martha Bennett
Thanks to Barry Hunt, Andy Balkham, Josh Clark, Chris Blanden
and Martha Bennett

CD produced by Josh Clark
Guitars: Joe Bennett (Fender Stratocaster and Taylor 414CE)
Bass: Chris Blanden (Fender Jazz)
Drums and Percussion: Josh Clark (DW drum kit)

Printed in the United States of America
by Vicks Lithograph and Printing Corporation

For all your guitar accessories, logon to www.musicroom.com

Your Guarantee of Quality
As publishers, we strive to produce every book to the highest
commercial standards.
The music has been freshly engraved and the book has been carefully
designed to minimize awkward page turns and to make playing from it
a real pleasure.
Throughout, the printing and binding have been planned to ensure
a sturdy, attractive publication which should give years of enjoyment.
If your copy fails to meet our high standards, please inform us and
we will gladly replace it.

www.musicsales.com

Contents

Introduction

Welcome to *The Complete Junior Guitarist*. This book is designed especially for younger guitar players (8–12), with a series of step-by-step lessons to develop techniques, strength and fluency on the guitar.

There are two ways you can use this book – with a teacher or on your own. A teacher will help you to develop proper "posture" (sitting position) and "fretting" (where to put your fingers), and may give advice on how to play the pieces. If you do use the book on your own, look carefully at the photos to make sure you are holding the guitar correctly, and your hands are in the right position. This will help you later on as you start to play more complicated music.

The book is divided into step-by-step lessons. Normally, a lesson would represent around one week of practice for a new player. However, every new guitarist learns at a different rate, so you may find that you do more than one lesson in a week, or you might take two or three weeks to finish a lesson.

Work at your own speed, and only move on to the next lesson when you feel really comfortable with the previous one.

Practice tips

• Play all of the examples slowly at first. It is better to play a piece of music accurately at a slow speed than to play it quickly with mistakes. Speed will always come with practice anyway.

• Once you start playing a new piece, keep it the same speed throughout. Don't speed up for the easy parts!

• Don't worry if you feel like a new piece is too difficult. Just look at the music one measure at a time, and work out which notes or chords need practice. You can put it all together later.

• Your fingertips may hurt slightly, particularly when you play chords. Don't worry – this is normal, and happens to every guitarist at first. Just take a break for a few hours.

• When you first start learning the guitar, around 20 minutes is usually enough time for a practice session.

• It's better to do lots of shorter practices than one long session.

Parts of the guitar

The **headstock** is at the far end of the neck; each string is attached here.

The **tuning pegs** are used to raise or lower the pitch of each string to keep the guitar in tune.

The **nut** is the small piece of plastic at the end of the neck. Each of the six strings passes through a groove in the nut.

The **neck** has between 17 and 24 frets. Necks are made of wood, although steel-string electric and acoustic guitar necks have a strengthening metal bar (called a *truss rod*) on the inside.

On the front of the neck is the **fingerboard** (sometimes called the **fretboard**).

The guitar has six **strings**, usually tuned (from thickest to thinnest) **E A D G B E**. The thinnest string is the "first string" and the thickest is the "sixth string."

Acoustic guitars have a **soundhole**. Electric guitars have one or more **pickups**.

Some guitars have a **pickguard** which protects the wood from damage, particularly if you use a pick.

The **bridge** anchors the strings at the opposite end of the guitar from the nut.

headstock

tuning pegs

nut

neck

fingerboard

soundhole

strings

bridge

Types of guitar

The steel-string **acoustic** guitar (sometimes just called the "acoustic" guitar) usually uses strings made of bronze and steel. For a beginner, it is the most difficult instrument to play because its strings are more difficult to press down onto the fingerboard. The acoustic guitar can be played with a pick or fingers.

The **classical** guitar usually has fewer frets than the acoustic or electric. Its strings are made of nylon, with the three bass strings adding a metal winding. For a beginner, it is the easiest of the three types to play because the nylon strings are less difficult to press onto the fingerboard. The classical guitar is usually played with the fingers, although some beginners use a pick.

The **electric** guitar requires an amplifier to be heard properly. It uses steel strings, which are usually lighter (thinner) than acoustic guitar strings. The electric guitar is usually played with a pick.

Left right?

All the examples in this book assume we're referring to a right-handed guitarist. If you're a left-handed player, you would hold the guitar the other way up and take the opposite position. Left-handed guitars are reverse-strung so that the thickest strings remain nearest the player's head; the thinnest strings are always closest to the floor.

The musical examples on the CD were played using either a steel-string guitar or an electric guitar. Some of the electric guitar parts also feature a "distortion" effect, which can be achieved using the amplifier or "effects pedals" into which you plug the guitar. You can play the pieces in this book on any type of guitar.

Accessories

Tuner

An electronic tuner has lights or a moving needle showing you when each string is exactly in tune.

Pick

A pick is held between the thumb and index finger of the picking hand, and typically gives a brighter "twang" to each note than fingers alone.

Pitch pipes

Pitch pipes are a simple wind instrument that provide the pitch of each open string of the guitar – E A D G B E. Blow into each one and compare the sound you hear with each open string of the guitar.

Capo

A capo is a movable nut that raises the pitch of all of the open strings by one or more frets' worth. You don't need a capo to work through this book, although you might start to use one when you begin to learn more chords.

Strings

There are three types of guitar string – electric, classical and acoustic. They normally come in sets of six. Ideally you should change your strings all at the same time, because a brand new string is noticeably louder than an older one.

Cases and gig bags

There are three types of cases – soft cases (a cloth bag for the guitar), gig bags (which contain padding to protect the guitar further) and hard cases (wooden or plastic cases with padded lining inside for maximum protection). If you travel or walk around with your guitar you should consider a gig bag or hard case.

Tuning your guitar

Before every practice session you should tune your instrument.
The guitar is tuned (from low to high) **E A D G B E**.

There are three ways to tune the guitar. For each method, you should pluck the string, and tighten its tuning peg if the string is too low-sounding ("flat"), or loosen it if the string is too high-sounding ("sharp").

1 Using a piano or keyboard

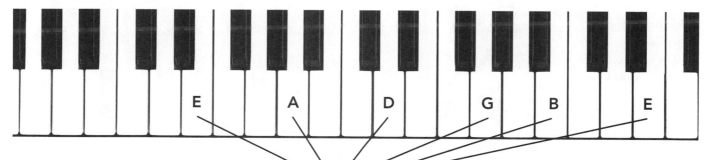

Play a note on the keyboard (or use pitch pipes), then play the corresponding open string. If the string sounds lower than the piano note, tighten its tuning peg until they sound the same. If the string sounds higher than the piano note, loosen the peg.

2 Using an electronic tuner

Electronic tuners will show you, using a light or moving needle, whether the string is sharp or flat when you play it.

3 Tuning the guitar to itself

This is the least reliable method for a beginner, but it is useful if you do not have access to a keyboard or tuner. Fret the sixth string at the 5th fret, and play it followed by the adjacent open fifth string. They should have the same pitch. If the open fifth string is higher than the fretted note, it is sharp, so loosen its peg until the notes sound the same. If the open string is lower, it is flat, so tighten its peg.

Repeat this process for each pair of strings – sixth/fifth, fifth/fourth, fourth/third, third/second, and second/first. Each time, fret the string at the fifth fret, except for the third/second string pair, when you should use the fourth fret.

If you don't have access to a keyboard or pitch pipes, use the tuning notes on Track 1 of this book's CD.

Holding your guitar

Folk/country position
Most acoustic guitar players use this posture because it makes strumming easier, and is comfortable for long practice sessions. If you find it easier, you can cross your legs and put the guitar on your right knee: this can help to stop it from sliding forward.

Classical position
This is more commonly used by classical guitarists, who sometimes also use a footstool to raise the guitar to the best position.

Fingerboard hand
Your fingerboard hand (that's your left hand if you're a right-handed player) should have its thumb in the center of the back of the neck. This will help your fingers to move more fluently around the fingerboard, and will make your chords sound more clearly.

One finger per fret!
All of the music in this book uses notes at the 1st, 2nd, and 3rd fret positions. These frets should be covered by the first, second and third fingers of your fingerboard hand. This will help you to develop strength in each finger equally, and will eventually enable you to play faster.

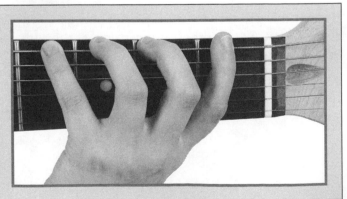

In performances, electric guitar players usually stand up and use a guitar strap; classical and acoustic players often sit down.

How to read music

Notation means any music that is written down. One of the most common types of notation is known as "treble clef"; it is identified by the swirl-shaped symbol on the left of each line (or "system") of music.

Treble clef notation

In treble clef notation, the open E string (the thinnest one on the guitar) is written in the top space. The open B string (the second thinnest) is written on the middle line. You'll learn other notes as you work through the lessons in this book.

Here's an example of the first three notes of *Three Blind Mice*. The first note (open E) starts in the top space, then descends to the line below (the note D), ending on the next space down (the note C).

Tablature or TAB

Tablature, or TAB for short, is a system for showing fingerboard positions as fret numbers. The six lines represent the guitar's six strings (the thinnest string of the guitar is the top line of the TAB). TAB is very helpful while you're learning the positions of the notes, but it doesn't show you any timing information (how long each note should last, and when you should play it). So normally you would read the treble clef, and use the TAB just to check that you're at the correct fret.

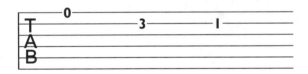

Rhythms and note values

This book uses four different types of notes.

A **quarter note** lasts for one beat.

A **half note** lasts for two beats.

A **whole note** lasts for four beats.

An **eighth note** lasts for half a beat – so you can play two of them in the time it takes to count one beat of the music.

When two or more eighth notes appear together, their stems are connected with a "beam."

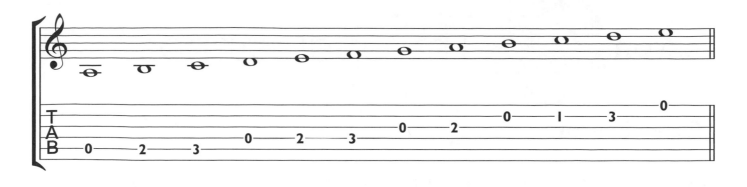

Here are all the musical notes you will play in this book, shown as treble clef and TAB.
You will learn them a few at a time, so don't worry about playing them all for now.

Like all guitar music, chords can be written in TAB or treble clef notation. More commonly, they are written as vertical "fretboxes," like this:

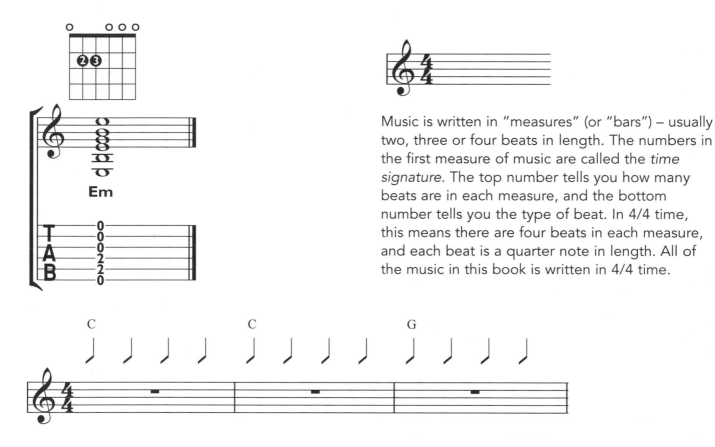

Music is written in "measures" (or "bars") – usually two, three or four beats in length. The numbers in the first measure of music are called the *time signature*. The top number tells you how many beats are in each measure, and the bottom number tells you the type of beat. In 4/4 time, this means there are four beats in each measure, and each beat is a quarter note in length. All of the music in this book is written in 4/4 time.

When you have learned a chord, usually it is not notated at all – its name is simply written above the music. Sometimes the music will include rhythm notation showing the timing of each chord. In this case, the chord part is notated in quarter notes, meaning that each strum would last for one beat.
In this example, the guitarist would play a C chord until the chord changes to G in the third measure.

If you're unsure of a note when you see it in a lesson, just turn back to this page to check its name and fingerboard position.

Lesson 1 The open strings

"Open Season"

This exercise uses only your picking hand (for right-handed guitarists, this is your right hand).
You can use the thumb or a pick to pluck each string.

The chords written above the music can be played by your teacher, or you can play along to the backing track.

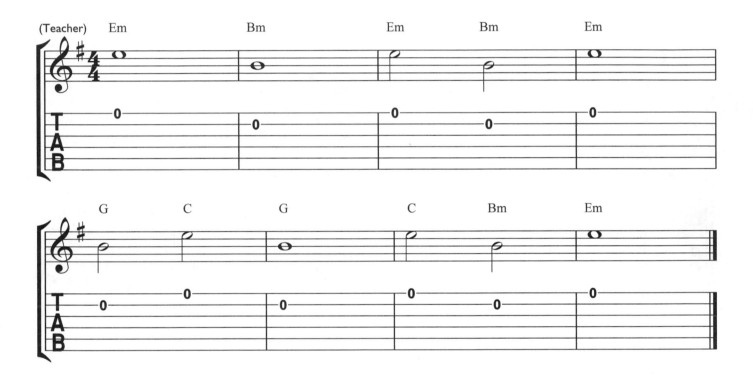

Listen to the full version on the CD so you can learn how each piece sounds.
Then try playing it yourself slowly.

When you can play it at full speed, play along with the teacher's guitar part.

"Crossing Over"

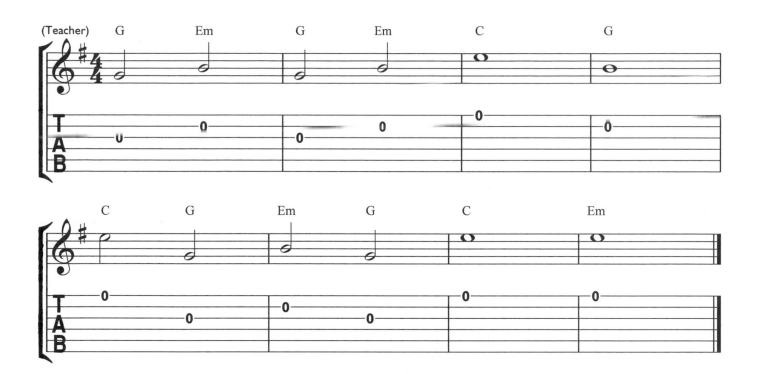

This piece uses the three highest-sounding (and thinnest) open strings – the **E**, **B** and **G** strings.

The most difficult part of this piece is picking the G string after the E string, avoiding playing the B string in between.

CD Tracks

2 Open Season full version
3 Open Season teacher's part
4 Crossing Over full version
5 Crossing Over teacher's part
6 You're The One full version
7 You're The One teacher's part

15

"You're The One"

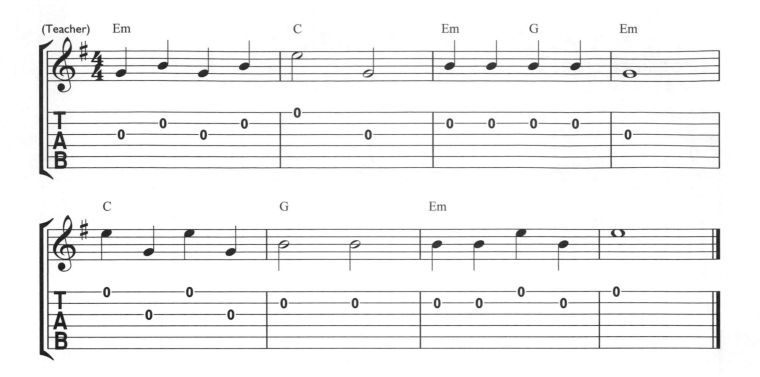

You'll hear from the CD that the notes in this piece seem to be faster. That's because we're using a quarter note. Quarter notes are worth one beat (a quarter of a bar in "four-four time").

Lesson 2 Fretted notes

The guitar has six open notes (from thickest to thinnest, these are **E, A, D, G, B** and **E** – the thinnest E is called the "first" string, B is the "second" string and so on). All other notes can be produced by "fretting" – pressing a finger onto the fingerboard slightly behind the fret.

In this lesson, we're going to use three fretted notes – **A**, **C** and **D**.

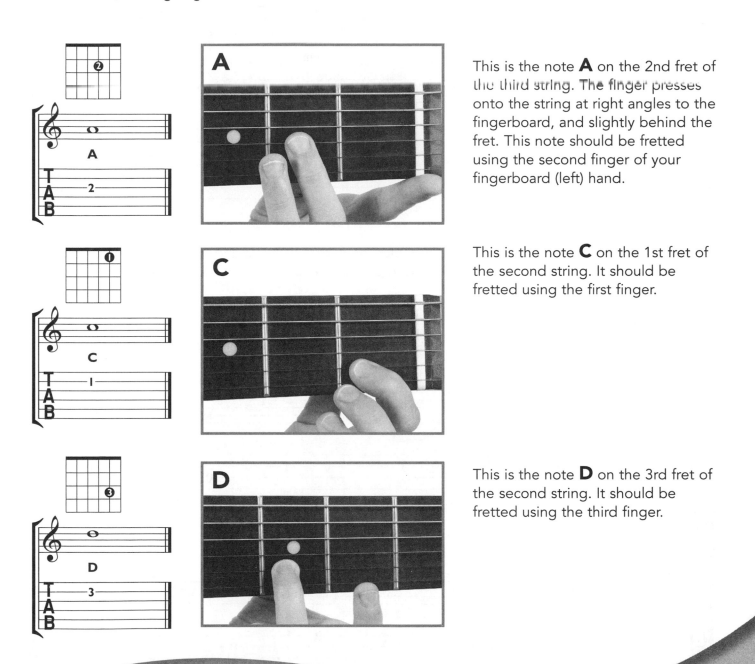

This is the note **A** on the 2nd fret of the third string. The finger presses onto the string at right angles to the fingerboard, and slightly behind the fret. This note should be fretted using the second finger of your fingerboard (left) hand.

This is the note **C** on the 1st fret of the second string. It should be fretted using the first finger.

This is the note **D** on the 3rd fret of the second string. It should be fretted using the third finger.

Tips for playing fretted notes
- Press onto the string slightly behind the fret.
- Press at right angles (straight down) onto the fingerboard.
- Don't push or pull the string sideways while fretting – this will make it go sharp (out of tune).
- Use "one finger per fret" – so your first finger should press at the 1st fret, your second finger the 2nd fret, and your third finger the 3rd fret. This will enable you to play more smoothly, and will develop strength in all your fingers equally.

"Keep It Clean"

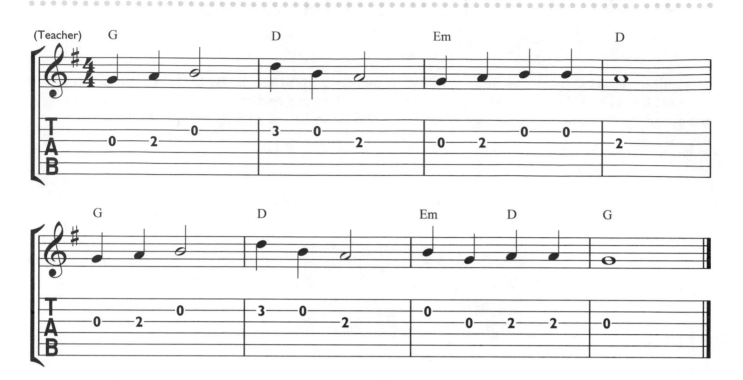

This piece includes the fretted notes A and D, plus the open G and B strings from the previous lesson. Use the thumb, or a downstroke with the pick, to pluck each note.

"Cleaner Still"

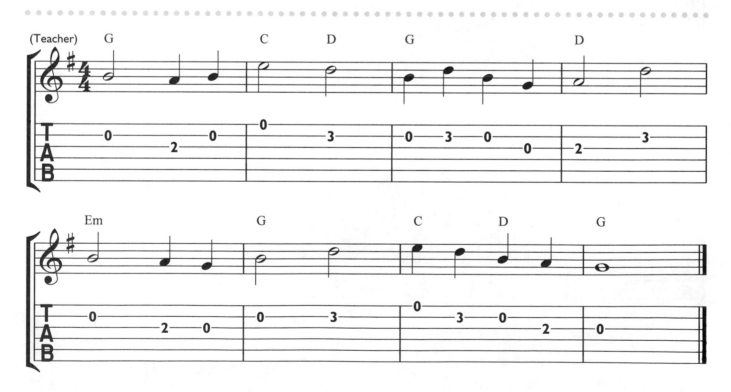

Here, we're using the fretted A and D, plus all three of the open strings (G, B and E) from Lesson 1. Measure 4 may take a little more practice because you need to play two fretted notes together, clearly and cleanly.

"Dark Dreams"

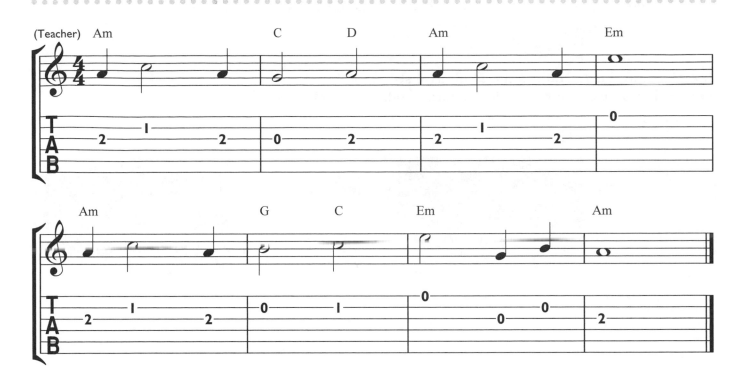

Dark Dreams is in a "minor key," meaning the melody has a sadder, more somber sound. It introduces a new fretted note – C at the 1st fret of the second string.

Our CD version is performed in a rock style, using an electric guitar and a distortion effect.

CD Tracks

8 Keep It Clean full version
9 Keep It Clean teacher's part
10 Cleaner Still full version
11 Cleaner Still teacher's part
12 Dark Dreams full version (electric guitar with distortion)
13 Dark Dreams teacher's part

Lesson 3 The fourth string

The pieces in this lesson use the **D** (fourth) string.
They will also help you to develop accuracy with your picking hand.

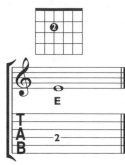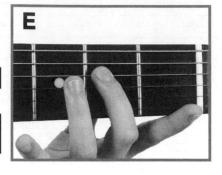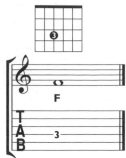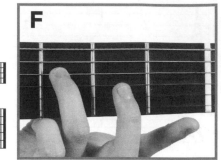

"Jazzy C"

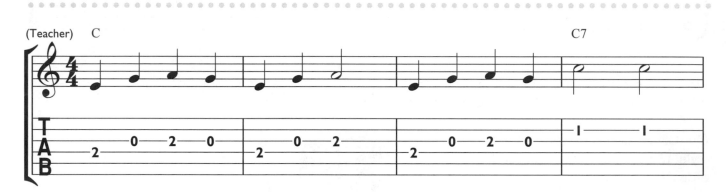

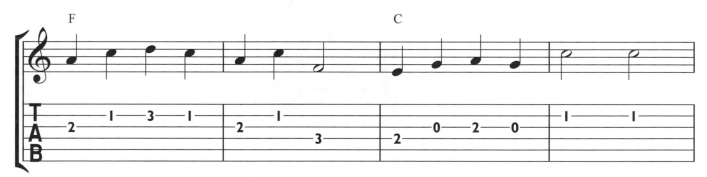

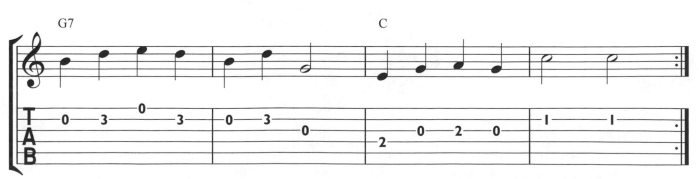

Despite the title, this piece is actually played in a blues style. Blues music is often arranged, as here, in sections lasting 12 bars. You'll notice that there is a double barline with two dots at the end of the music. This is a "repeat sign" and it means you should go back to the beginning; i.e., the piece should be played twice.

"Miss De Minor"

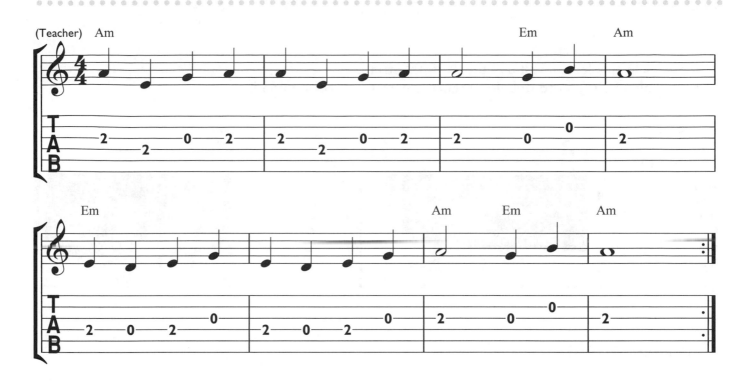

Here is an eight-bar piece using the fretted notes A and E, both played at the 2nd fret. The CD version is played with a pick on an acoustic guitar, with a backing track played in a reggae style. As before, there is a repeat sign at the end of the music.

When you see this sign (double barline with two vertical dots) it means you should play the music twice – so go back to the beginning without a pause and play the whole piece through again.

Classical guitarists pluck the strings using their thumb and fingers; electric guitarists generally use a pick. For these first few lessons, pluck each note with your thumb or with a pick. We will begin to explore "fingerstyle" in Lesson 9.

CD Tracks

14 Jazzy C full version
15 Jazzy C teacher's part
16 Miss De Minor full version
17 Miss De Minor teacher's part

Lesson 4 The fifth string

The pieces in this lesson will use the **A** (fifth) string.
They will also help you to develop accuracy with your picking hand.

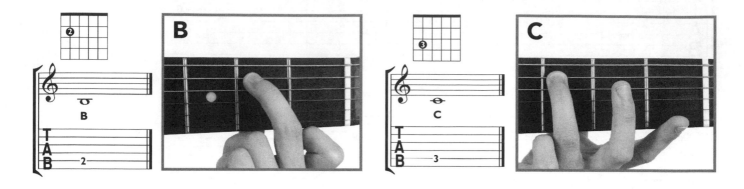

C major scale

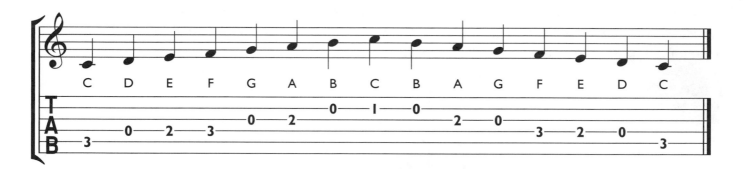

| C | D | E | F | G | A | B | C | B | A | G | F | E | D | C |

These eight notes form a one-octave scale, starting on C on the fifth (**A**) string and ending on C one octave higher on the second (**B**) string.

Scales are useful for learning the note names, and also for developing fluency and finger strength.

You can use any notes from a scale to make up your own melodies – this is called "improvising."

A natural minor scale

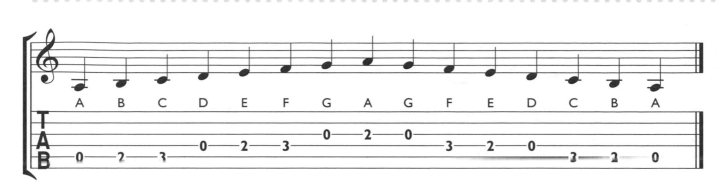

Minor scales, like minor melodies, have a darker, sadder musical sound. This A natural minor scale begins on the open fifth (**A**) string and ends on a 2nd fret A on the third (**G**) string.

With all scales, you should aim to play them evenly, so that each note lasts the same length of time.

The next two pieces include **eighth notes**. They last for half a beat, so for every "count" of the music you should play two notes.

Listen to this lesson's CD examples while looking at the page, and you'll see and hear where the "faster" notes arrive.

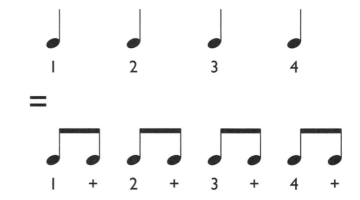

18 **C major scale** ascending and descending
19 **A natural minor scale** ascending and descending

"Count Juan"

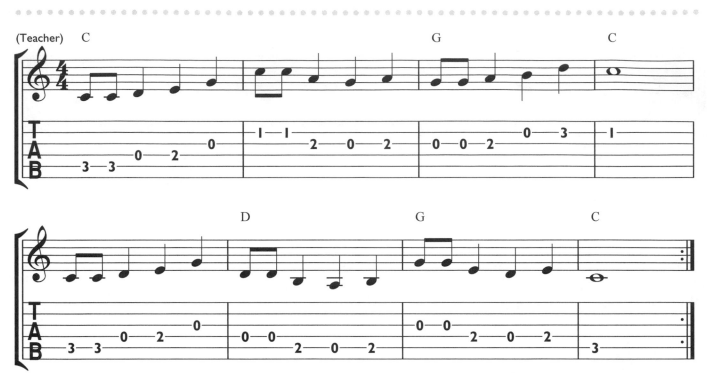

The first two notes of each measure are eighth notes, followed by three ordinary quarter notes. So the rhythm of the first measure, for example, could be spoken as "da-da daaa daaa daaa."

"Kantu"

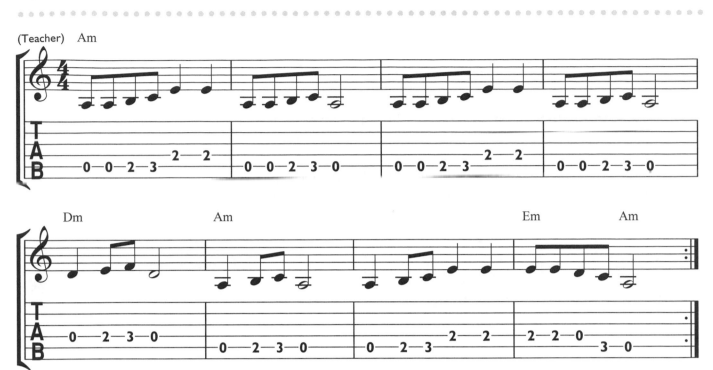

Here, the first *four* notes of the first measure are eighth notes, so you would speak these notes as "da-da-da-da daaa daaa."

For the second half of the piece, the rhythm changes so that each measure starts with a quarter note followed by two eighth notes followed by a half note. So, the rhythm would be "daaa da-da daaaaaaaa."

20 Count Juan full version
21 Count Juan teacher's part
22 Kantu full version (electric guitar with distortion)
23 Kantu teacher's part

Lesson 5 Riffs and rests

By now you've played a variety of short and long notes: whole notes, half notes, quarter notes, and eighth notes.

In this lesson, we're going to play some pieces that use *rests* – gaps in the music where you don't play anything at all.

Two of the pieces in this lesson use "riffs" – short musical phrases that are repeated several times in a piece of music.

Riffs appear in many styles of music, but they are particularly common in rock and pop because the constant repetition of each riff helps the audience to remember the song.

A whole-note rest lasts for four beats

A half-note rest lasts for two beats

A quarter-note rest lasts for one beat

An eighth-note rest lasts for half a beat

Note that TAB notation does not usually include rests or note lengths, so you will need to look at the treble clef above to see where the rests are.

As you progress through the book, you are encouraged to look at the treble clef rather than the TAB because it will give you more information about how the piece should be played.

"Sea Country"

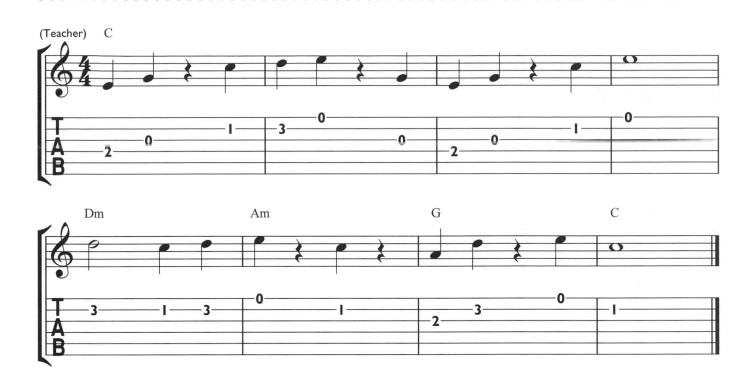

Sea Country is a lullaby-style piece and there is a quarter-note rest on the third beat of each measure. In measure 6, the rests are on the second and fourth beats. The CD version features an electric guitar playing the melody and an acoustic guitar playing the teacher's part.

24 Sea Country full version (electric and acoustic guitar)
25 Sea Country teacher's part

"White Knight"

The notes in *White Knight* are faster eighth notes, but the quarter-note rest is the same as in *Sea Country*. The CD version is recorded in a European folk style.

"Eighth Day"

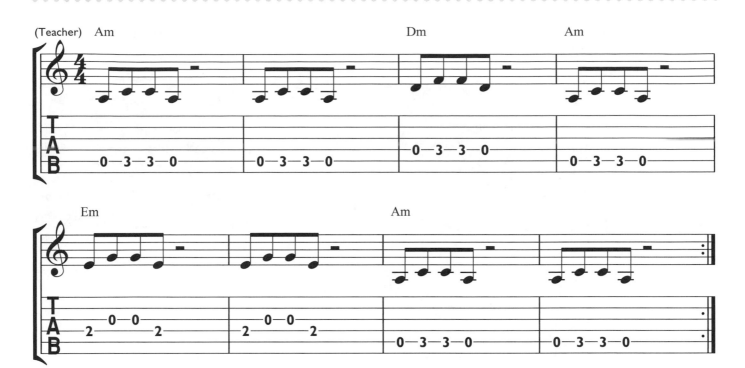

Each measure of *Eighth Day* is rhythmically the same – a group of four eighth notes, followed by a half-note rest. The piece has a fast rock feel. Note the repeat sign, showing that the music should be played twice.

The CD version features drums and electric bass, but it can be played with two guitars – the teacher's chord part is written above the treble clef notation.

CD Tracks

26 White Knight full version
27 White Knight teacher's part
28 Eighth Day full version (electric guitar and band)
29 Eighth Day teacher's part

Lesson **6** Introducing chords

When guitarists play more than one note at the same time, this is called a *chord*. The guitar, being a six-stringed instrument, can play chords containing up to six notes.

In this lesson you're going to learn three new chords – simple **G**, simple **C** and simple **E minor** (usually written as **Em**).

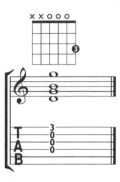

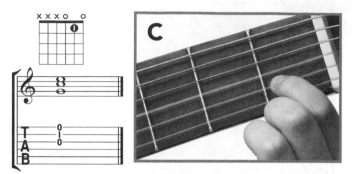

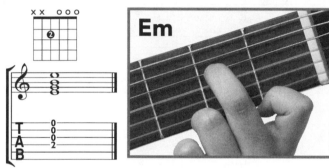

How to play chords

Play each chord as a single downstrum with your thumb or pick. Fretting the notes in a chord is the easy part – what is more difficult is to ensure that your fretting finger does not prevent any of the open strings from ringing.

To check that your chord is played correctly, try strumming it once, then pick every note of the chord one by one to check that you don't hear that dull "thud" of your finger accidentally stopping the string.

You will notice that these chords have an **X** written above some of the strings. These represent strings that should not be played. Strings with an **O** above them should be strummed as an open string.

For the moment, strum each chord with a single downstroke of the pick or the thumb. The pick will make a "brighter" sound and the thumb a "warmer" sound. All of the examples on the CD have been played with a pick.

Here are three new pieces of music designed to help you to explore chords. We've included all of the melody notes too, which you are welcome to try separately.

To play the chord part, you should simply read the chord names above the music and strum one downstroke to every beat of the music.

The CD contains a version of both parts together so you can hear how the whole piece should sound, as well as a version of the melody only (so you can play the chords).

"September Sunshine"

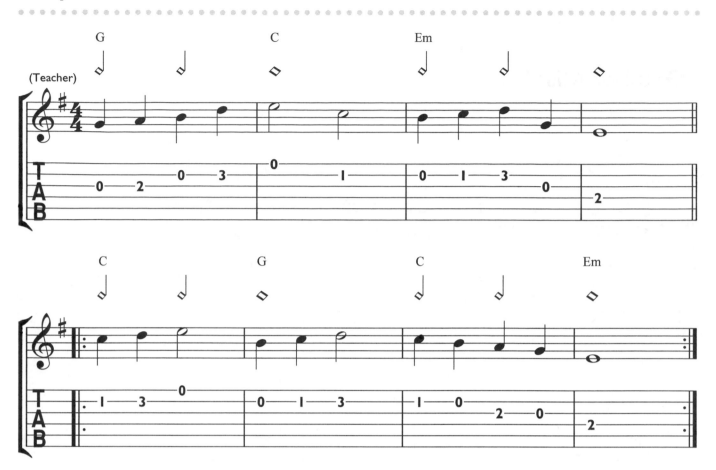

Here, the chords are written as rhythm guitar notation. The teacher (or CD) plays the melody part, and you should strum the chords using the rhythms shown above the notation. Use a downward strum for each chord. You'll see that there are repeat marks in both directions – this means you should play the last four measures twice.

Once you've mastered the chords and can play along to the teacher's (electric guitar) part on the CD, you can try playing the melody yourself over the full track as extra practice.

CD Tracks

30 **September Sunshine** full version
31 **September Sunshine** teacher's part (melody and band)
32 **October Mist** full version
33 **October Mist** teacher's part

"October Mist"

All of the rests we used in the previous lesson can equally be applied to chords. To stop the second strummed chord from ringing out too long during the rest, gently touch the strings with the side of your strumming hand. The recorded version uses an acoustic guitar for the chords and an electric guitar for the melody part.

These recordings are different from the ones you've heard so far, because you will now be playing the chord parts. The teacher's part has the chords removed so you can play the strumming part.

Lesson 7 More chords

The three chords you have learned so far use only one fretted note played with one finger of the fretting hand.

The chords in this lesson are more difficult because they use two or three fingers, so all the notes have to be fretted equally firmly and accurately at the same time.

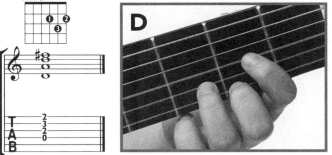

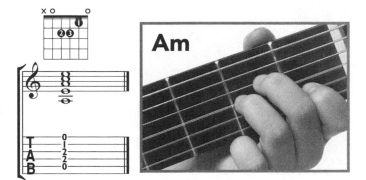

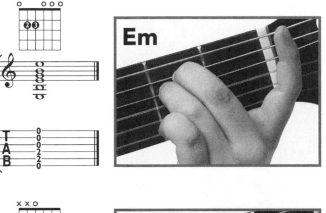

Practice each chord on its own lots of times, then try changing between one chord and the next slowly. Eventually, you will be able to change between chords without leaving a gap in the flow of the music.

Once you can do this, you'll be ready to play along with the CD.

We looked at "simple Em" in the previous lesson. This version uses all six strings and can sound very full and loud. The other two chords – Am and D – are new, and require three fingers of the fingerboard hand.

It is normal for this lesson to take quite a long time to work through, so don't worry if you find these chords difficult at first – particularly the Am and D shapes.

"Trial Run"

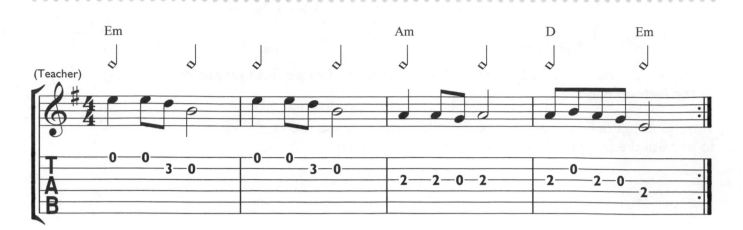

Strum each chord using a thumb or pick downstroke for a count of two beats.
To play the D chord, strum four strings only, leaving the two thickest bass strings untouched.

The Am is a five-string chord, and the Em a six-string chord.

"School's In"

Now we're strumming different-length chords. Measure 1 is a whole note, lasting the full four beats.
Measure 2 uses half notes as before. Measure 3 uses quarter notes – that's four strums per measure.

"Merlin's Phoenix"

To play the "rhythm guitar" (chords) part in this English folk-style tune, you will need to mix up your strumming rhythms. Listen carefully to the CD version of the chord part while reading the rhythm notation underneath the chords – this will also help to develop your sight-reading skills.

CD Tracks

34 Trial Run full version
35 Trial Run teacher's part
36 School's In full version
37 School's In teacher's part
38 Merlin's Phoenix full version
39 Merlin's Phoenix teacher's part

Lesson 8 Strumming

Everything you have learned so far about rhythm (i.e., short and long notes) can be applied to chords.

So, you can strum a single chord and let it ring out for a whole note, or strum a quarter note on every beat. Mixing up combinations of short and long strums makes chord rhythms sound more interesting.

In this lesson, you'll play some pieces that use different note lengths, using all of the chords from the previous two lessons. As before, we've included all of the music for both guitar parts (melody and chords) – you should concentrate on the chord (rhythm) part, but feel free to try the melody part later.

Chord rhythms
Sometimes guitar music includes rhythm notation to show how the composer wants you to strum the chords. We've included it for all of the music in this chapter.

When you play rhythm guitar, you are encouraged to make up your own strumming-hand rhythms. Professional guitarists do this all the time, particularly in rock and pop music. Remember to make sure each chord rings out clearly when you strum – so you'll have to concentrate on both hands at the same time!

"Street Sweeper"

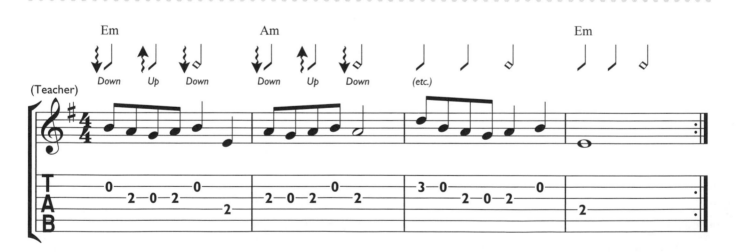

This rock piece uses the chords E minor and A minor (written as Em and Am).
The strumming hand should follow the same pattern throughout (down-up, down).

36

Strumming exercises

Downstrokes

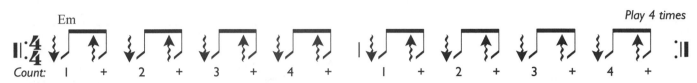

First, practice downstrokes. This exercise includes three strums per chord, and a rest on the fourth beat of each measure, giving you a bit more time to change chords. Note that each chord in this exercise requires you to strum a different number of strings. The E minor in measure 1 uses all six strings; the A minor in measure 2 leaves out the sixth string; the D in measure 3 leaves out the sixth and fifth strings – so make sure you only strum the strings you actually need.

Downstrokes and upstrokes

This exercise alternates down- and upstrokes. Practice moving your wrist and arm so that the upstrokes are the same speed and volume as the downstrokes. For now, we're just using a single E minor chord throughout.

Changing the rhythm

Now try varying your rhythms to create a more interesting part. This exercise uses the same strumming pattern throughout (down, down-up-down) followed by a rest, during which you should change to the next chord.

Half-bar changes

Chords can change anywhere in a measure, not just at the start. In this exercise, the chords change every two beats (every half bar) and each chord is played with a down-up-down strumming pattern.

"Espresso"

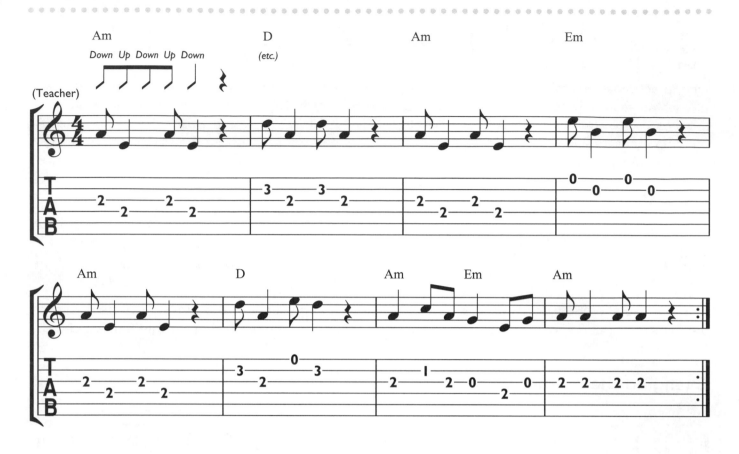

Here, you're using a faster (eighth-note) strumming pattern (down-up-down-up down), and introducing a new chord – D. There is a one-beat rest at the end of each measure, giving you some time to move your fingers into the next chord shape.

You may find it helpful to flatten your strumming hand gently on the strings to stop them ringing during this rest, while your fretting hand finds the next chord. The CD version features electric guitar playing the melody and the acoustic guitar playing your part – the chords.

Strumming tip
Make sure you only strum the strings in the chord – so if you're playing a D chord you should only strum the four thinnest strings, leaving the others untouched. This will take a lot of practice, particularly when you're strumming the upstroke.

Lesson 9 Fingerstyle

So far, you've sounded all of the notes using your thumb or a pick.

In this lesson, you're going to try picking the third, second and first (thinnest) strings with the first, second and third fingers of your picking hand. Normally, in fingerstyle guitar playing, the thumb of the picking hand covers the fourth, fifth and sixth strings, and the fingers cover one each of the three remaining strings.

Hand position for fingerstyle

This is the correct starting position for fingerstyle guitar playing. Usually, each finger plays only the notes on its own string, so try to have your fingers ready in this position at all times.

Classical guitar fingerstyle notation
- The thumb (labeled **p** in guitar notation) plays all notes on the three bass (thickest) strings.
- The first/index finger (labeled **i** in guitar notation) rests on the third string.
- The second/middle finger (labeled **m** in guitar notation) rests on the second string.
- The third/ring finger (labeled **a** in guitar notation) rests on the first string.

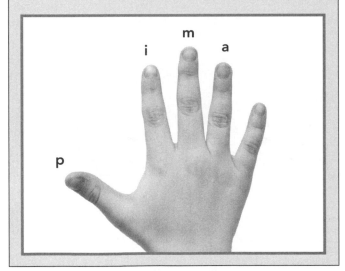

Fingerstyle position for acoustic and classical guitar

Fingerstyle position for electric guitar

Fingerstyle technique is often used in folk and classical guitar music; pick technique is more common in rock and pop styles.

"Westbury Horse"

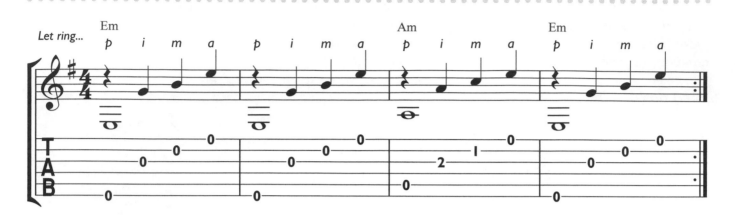

This is a piece for solo fingerstyle guitar – so it does not include a teacher's part. The thumb should pluck the bass note at the start of every measure, then the fingers should play one note each on the third, second and first strings.

Above the score is the performance instruction "let ring," meaning that all notes should ring throughout the bar. The bars of A minor may take a little more practice, because you will need to concentrate on fretting the notes properly at the same time as picking the strings in the right order.

"On The Nose"

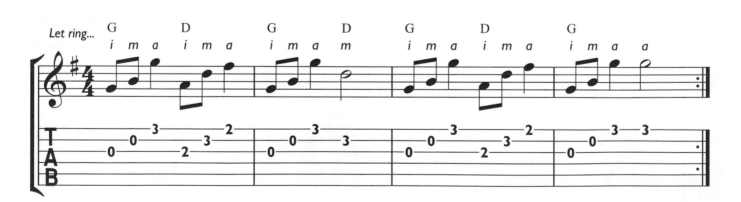

In this piece the chords change in half bars – so your fretting hand will need to change chords every two beats.

As with all the faster examples, you should practice this piece slowly before building up to speed or playing along with the CD.

"Mr. Preview's Order"

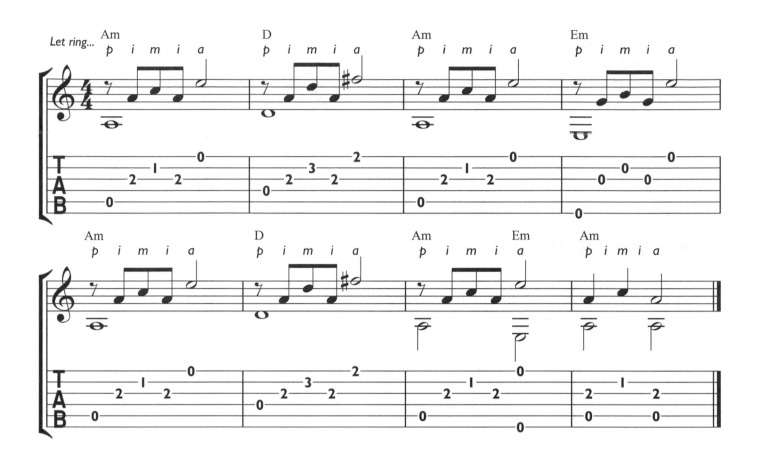

The fingers always cover the same strings, but not necessarily in the same order. In this example, the fingers play the following pattern – **p**, **i**, **m**, **i**, **a** (thumb, index finger, middle finger, index finger, ring finger).

This is easier to see when you look at the TAB. As before, let the notes ring for the whole measure, and use the thumb to pluck the bass note at the start of each bar.

52 Westbury Horse full version (solo fingerstyle)
53 On The Nose full version (solo fingerstyle)
54 Mr. Preview's Order full version (solo fingerstyle)

Lesson 10 All together

In this final lesson, you're going to play two pieces of music that bring together everything you've learned so far:

- Playing open notes
- Playing fretted notes
- Playing chords
- Note values and rhythms
- Strumming

The first piece is designed to be played fingerstyle; the second requires a pick.
By now, you may be starting to develop your own "style."

A guitarist's style can be a combination of your tastes (the music you like to listen to) and your technique (how you like to play). Generally, if you prefer to listen to rock and pop music, you will be more likely to develop pick technique; if you prefer to listen to classical and folk music, you will be more likely to use fingerstyle.

"Trees In The Park"

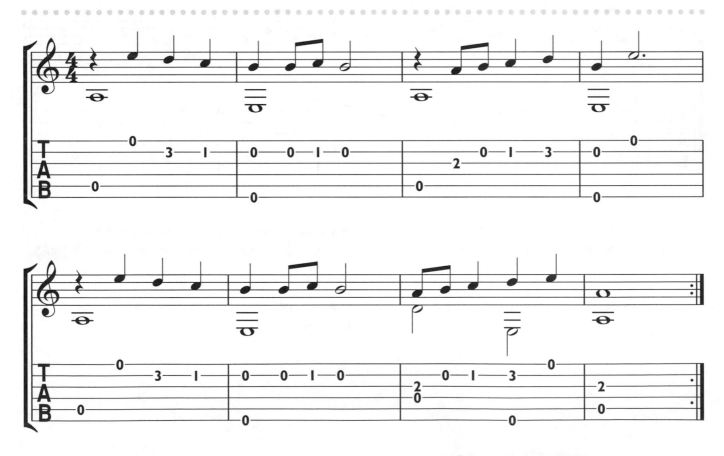

This classical-style guitar piece should be played fingerstyle. It uses all six strings of the guitar.
You will need to pluck the bass notes with the thumb at the same time as some of the melody notes.
Your picking hand may take some time to develop this coordination, so be patient.

"Moles In The Basement"

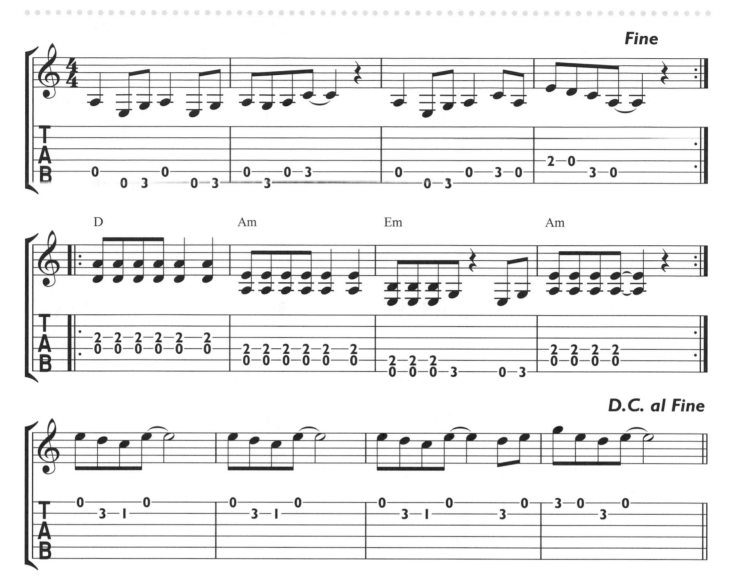

This rock-style piece is best played with a pick and, like all of the pieces in the book, can be performed on an electric or acoustic guitar. It uses most of the notes you have learned so far, and introduces a new note – G on the sixth string (played at the 3rd fret).

At the end of the notation you'll see the instruction **D.C. al Fine**. "D.C." stands for *Da Capo* ("from the head" in Italian) and means you should go back to the beginning. The phrase *al Fine* (pronounced "Al Finee") means you should stop playing when you next see the instruction *Fine*.

CD Tracks
55 Trees In The Park full version
56 Moles In The Basement full version
57 Moles In The Basement teacher's part

43

Chord library

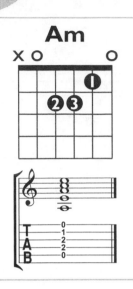

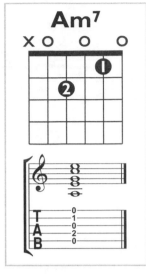

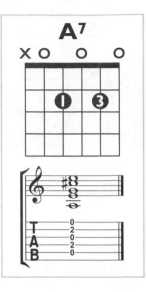

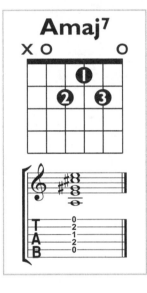

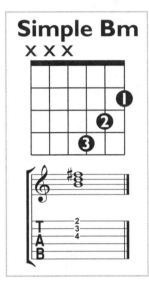

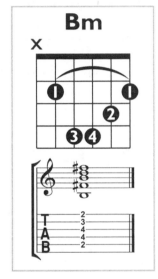

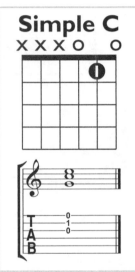

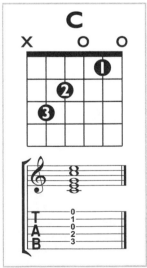

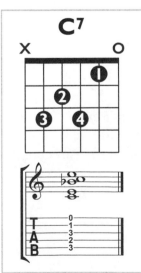

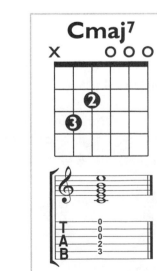

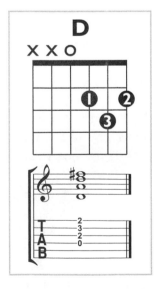

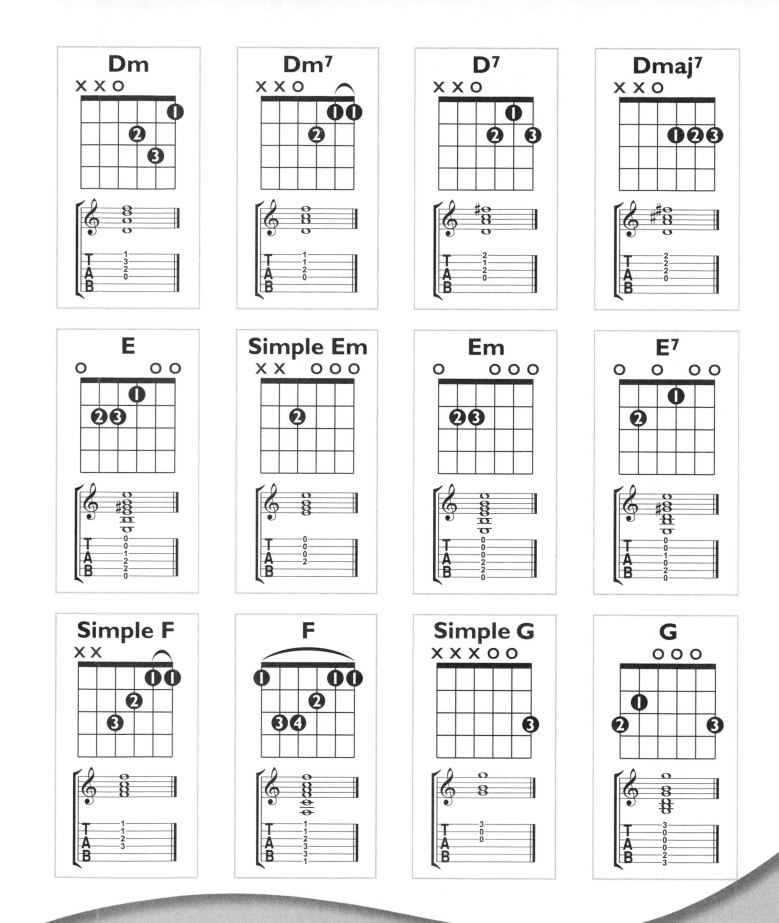

Glossary

Amp: short for amplifier. Electric guitars need to be plugged into an amplifier to be heard properly.

Arpeggio: playing the notes of a chord one by one.

Bar: see *measure*.

Cable: a cord for connecting the electric guitar to the amplifier.

Chord: more than one note played at the same time.

Clean sound: any guitar sound without distortion.

Da Capo: Italian for "from the head," meaning you should go back to the beginning of the music.

Distortion: a "fuzzy" sounding effect, used most often on electric guitar sounds, produced by the amplifier or a separate distortion pedal.

Eighth note: a note lasting for half a beat.

Fine: Italian for "finish" meaning you should stop playing if you see this phrase after you've played past a section which contains the words "al Fine" ("to the finish").

Fingerboard: the flat side of the neck, where you fret the notes.

Fingerstyle: playing the guitar without a pick.

Frets: the metal strips on the neck.

Half note: a note lasting for two beats.

Headstock: the end part of the guitar, where the tuning pegs can be found.

Interval: the musical space between two notes. Tones and semitones are intervals.

Major chord: a chord made from the root, third and fifth of the major scale. Many people think that major chords sound bright and happy.

Measure: a number of beats – usually two, three or four – that divide up the music into equal-length sections. Also known as a *bar*.

Minor chord: a chord made from the root, third and fifth of the minor scale. Many people think that minor chords sound dark and sad.

Notation: written or printed music. The guitar uses treble clef notation.

Nut: the white plastic string holder between the headstock and the fingerboard.

Nylon-string: any guitar that uses strings that have a nylon core. Almost always refers to classical guitars.

Open string: the note produced when you pluck a string without fretting a note on the fingerboard.

Pick: a small flexible piece of plastic that is used to pluck the strings, most commonly on a steel-string acoustic or electric guitar.

Pickup: a magnetic device that sits under electric guitar strings so that they can be amplified.

Quarter note: a note lasting for one beat.

Rest: a space in the music where you don't play anything.

Reverb: an echo-like effect that makes your guitar sound like it's in a church or large room.

Saddle: the part of the bridge that the strings go over at the opposite end of the neck from the nut.

Selector: a switch on the top of an electric guitar enabling you to select different pickups to change the guitar tone.

Semitone: the smallest space between two different-pitched notes, equivalent to one fret's worth. Also known as a half step or half tone.

Soundboard: the flat area of an acoustic steel-string or classical guitar that contains the soundhole.

Soundhole: the hole in the center of an acoustic or classical guitar, which produces most of the sound.

Staff: the five lines on which musical notes appear.

Steel-string: any guitar that uses strings that have a steel core. Can refer to acoustic or electric guitars.

Strumming: moving your pick or fingers down or up across more than one string at the same time.

Tablature: form of guitar notation where numbers are used to show fret positions for each note. TAB for short.

Time signature: numbers at the beginning of the notation, telling you the number and type of beat used in the music.

Tone: two semitones – a pitch equivalent to two frets' worth. Also known as a whole step or whole tone.

Top: the face of the guitar – the side that has the soundhole or pickups.

Treble clef: the scroll-shaped symbol that appears at the start of guitar notation. The center of the scroll shows you where to find the note G.

Truss rod: metal bar inside the neck of steel-string acoustic and electric guitars.

Tuner: electronic device that can identify the pitch of a guitar string when you play it, helping you to tell if the guitar is correctly in tune.

Whole note: a note lasting for four beats.

CD Track Listing

1	**Tuning Notes**		**30**	**September Sunshine** Full
2	**Open Season** Full		**31**	**September Sunshine** Teacher
3	**Open Season** Teacher		**32**	**October Mist** Full
4	**Crossing Over** Full		**33**	**October Mist** Teacher
5	**Crossing Over** Teacher		**34**	**Trial Run** Full
6	**You're The One** Full		**35**	**Trial Run** Teacher
7	**You're The One** Teacher		**36**	**School's In** Full
8	**Keep It Clean** Full		**37**	**School's In** Teacher
9	**Keep It Clean** Teacher		**38**	**Merlin's Phoenix** Full
10	**Cleaner Still** Full		**39**	**Merlin's Phoenix** Teacher
11	**Cleaner Still** Teacher		**40**	**Street Sweeper** Full
12	**Dark Dreams** Full		**41**	**Street Sweeper** Teacher
13	**Dark Dreams** Teacher		**42**	**Strumming downstrokes** Full
14	**Jazzy C** Full		**43**	**Strumming downstrokes** Teacher
15	**Jazzy C** Teacher		**44**	**Strumming downstrokes and upstrokes** Full
16	**Miss De Minor** Full		**45**	**Strumming downstrokes and upstrokes** Teacher
17	**Miss De Minor** Teacher			
18	**C major scale**		**46**	**Changing the rhythm** Full
19	**A natural minor scale**		**47**	**Changing the rhythm** Teacher
20	**Count Juan** Full		**48**	**Half-bar changes** Full
21	**Count Juan** Teacher		**49**	**Half-bar changes** Teacher
22	**Kantu** Full		**50**	**Espresso** Full
23	**Kantu** Teacher		**51**	**Espresso** Teacher
24	**Sea Country** Full		**52**	**Westbury Horse** Full
25	**Sea Country** Teacher		**53**	**On The Nose** Full
26	**White Knight** Full		**54**	**Mr. Preview's Order** Full
27	**White Knight** Teacher		**55**	**Trees In The Park** Full
28	**Eighth Day** Full		**56**	**Moles In The Basement** Full
29	**Eighth Day** Teacher		**57**	**Moles In The Basement** Teacher